The Quick Meats Cookbook

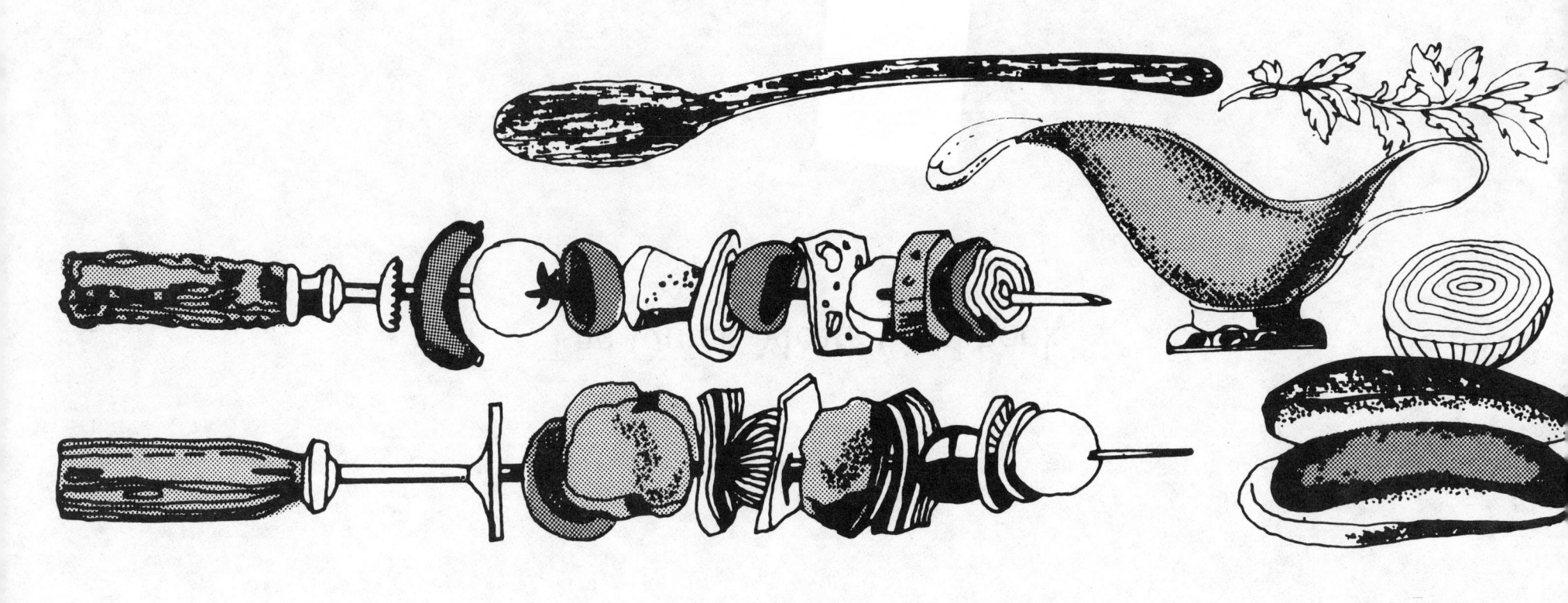

Illustrations by Lillian Langseth-Christensen

The Quick Meats Cookbook

Lillian Langseth-Christensen and Carol Sturm Smith

Walker and Company New York

ISBN: 0-8027-2462-0
Library of Congress Catalog Card Number: 67–23080

Printed in the United States of America

Designed by *Arlene Greco*

This Walker Large Print edition published in 1984.

TABLE OF CONTENTS

HOW TO USE THE BOOK

All of the recipes in this book take less than 30 minutes of cooking time, although a few marinate for several hours before the cooking process begins. The only exceptions will be in those cases where thick steaks are prepared, and guests ask for well-done meat.

(1) Read the recipe through.

(2) Prepare the ingredients.

(3) Have the meat at room temperature.

(4) Be acquainted with the basic information and cooking times on the steak charts, and the method for preparing scallopini.

(5) The proportions for seasoned flour: ½ cup flour, 1 tsp salt, ½ tsp pepper.

(6) All quick meats should be served on heated platters and served immediately, so have your table set and your guests ready for the meal.

BROILED STEAKS: The steak is cooked by dry heat, either on an electric unit, a gas flame or over hot coals or charcoal. Steaks can also be broiled in a hot pan on top of the stove, usually called pan broiling.

GRILLED STEAKS: The same as broiled steaks, but broiled on a hot grill or grid or gridiron. These steaks should show the crisscross pattern of the hot iron.

FOR BROILED STEAKS: Buy steaks at least 1 inch thick, and preferably thicker. Steaks that are too thin are apt to dry out and often are already overdone in the few minutes it takes to brown the surface.

FOR PAN BROILING STEAKS: Buy steaks from ½ to 1½ inches thick.

HOW LONG TO BROIL: Most recipes specify "to taste," meaning until the outside is nicely browned and the inside is rare, medium rare, medium, medium well or well done. Steaks that are cooked until well done are usually less juicy than those cooked only until rare, medium rare or medium.

FOR ALL STEAKS: Trim the meat. If there is an edge of fat left, it should be slashed in a few places to keep the steak from curling. Do not slash deeply into the meat.

Place the rack 2–3 inches from the heat, unless the steak is very thick, in which case the rack should be lowered until the top of the meat is 1–2 inches from the heat unit. Broil until the meat is brown. Season and turn and brown the second side. The first side will take a fraction longer than the second side.

The following times are for steak cuts broiled in a 350°F broiler, with the rack 2–3 inches from the heat. Time given is for total broiling time, so if 16 minutes are specified, allow 8½ minutes on the first side, 7½ on the second. Broiling times are for rare steaks; increase approximately 4 minutes in all for medium, 6–8 minutes in all for well done.

CLUB STEAKS	1 inch thick	12 minutes
	2 inches thick	28 minutes
FILLET STEAKS, FILET MIGNONS	1 inch thick	7 minutes
	2 inches thick	14 minutes
PORTERHOUSE STEAKS	1 inch thick	16 minutes
	2 inches thick	34 minutes
RIB STEAKS	1 inch thick	12 minutes
	2 inches thick	28 minutes

SIRLOIN STEAKS	1 inch thick	16 minutes
	2 inches thick	35 minutes
T-BONE STEAKS	1 inch thick	12 minutes
	2 inches thick	28 minutes
TOURNEDOS	1½ inches thick	10 minutes
	2½ inches thick	21 minutes

PAN-BROILED STEAKS: Pan broiling takes less time than broiling. The meat should be thinner. The following list of times also indicates minimum thickness for successful steaks. Times are for rare.

For medium pan-broiled steaks, add about a total of 4 minutes to cooking time.
For well-done pan-broiled steaks, broil until crisp.

CLUB STEAKS	½ inch thick	4 minutes
	1½ inches thick	16 minutes
FILLET STEAKS, FILET MIGNONS	1½ inches thick	10 minutes
PORTERHOUSE STEAKS	½ inch thick	6 minutes
	1½ inches thick	16 minutes

RIB STEAKS	1 inch thick	8 minutes
	1½ inches thick	14 minutes
SIRLOIN STEAKS	½ inch thick	6 minutes
	1½ inches thick	16 minutes
T-BONE STEAKS	½ inch thick	4 minutes
	1½ inches thick	16 minutes
TOURNEDOS	1½ inches thick	10 minutes

PAN FRIED STEAKS are the same as above, with a little butter, oil or fat added to the pan. The butter, oil or fat is heated to bubbling before the meat is added to the pan.

INFRA-RED BROILED STEAKS

Follow same general directions as for oven broiled steaks: Wipe steaks, slash the fat in several places and broil in the preheated broiler, about 3 inches from the heat unit, according to the following:

RARE STEAKS	1 inch thick	5–6 minutes per side
	1½ inches thick	6–7 minutes per side
	2 inches thick	12–14 minutes per side

MEDIUM STEAKS—Increase time by 1–2 minutes on each side.

WELL-DONE STEAKS—Double the time given for rare steaks.

STEAKS, SAUCES AND ACCOMPANIMENTS

A FEW RULES FOR BROILED AND PAN BROILED STEAKS

(1) Do not salt a steak before cooking, unless recipe specifies it.

(2) Wipe and dry the steak with a towel before cooking.

(3) Bring all steaks to room temperature before cooking.

(4) Turn steaks with tongs while cooking, not with a fork, which breaks the surface of the meat.

(5) Learn to recognize when the steak is done by the surface appearance or go by a timer rather than cutting into the meat, which allows juices to escape.

(6) If you must cut into the meat, make a small incision near the bone.

(7). Slash the fat around the meat to prevent curling, but avoid cutting into the meat itself.

(8) Allow half a pound of boneless steak per person; increase to a pound per person when the steaks contain a heavy bone.

(9) Serve steaks on very hot platters and plates—quick-cooked meats do not cook long enough to remain hot on cold plates.

(10) If guests prefer different degrees of "doneness" start the steaks that need to be well done before the others, so all are done at the same time if individual steaks or several steaks are being used.

THE MEAT FONDUES

Fondue was originally the family meal of Swiss mountain peasants, and was named for the single utensil in which it was cooked. Various districts provided various cheeses and the fondues were classified accordingly. Leftover meat was added to some of them and after a time the cheese was omitted and the meat alone remained. It is the quickest way of cooking meat, about 10 seconds, and also the friendliest, since everyone sits around the fondue pot and cooks his own meat while they count to ten.

FONDUE BOURGUIGNONNE

(1) Have butcher cut large cubes from thin end and scraps of beef filet to obtain:

2–3 lbs fillet of beef

(2) In fondue pot, bring to a boil on kitchen stove:

2–3 inches cooking oil
1 clove garlic

(3) Transfer boiling oil to fondue burner and adjust flame so that oil continues to simmer.

(4) Arrange meat on a platter. Each guest spears his own meat chunk on his fondue fork and holds it in the simmering oil for 10 seconds, or until browned to taste.

(5) The sizzling meat is then dipped into one of the following prepared sauces and eaten immediately:

1 cup tomato catsup
1 cup cold tartar sauce
1 cup warm Béarnaise sauce

16

½ cup mustard
½ cup horseradish

(6) Buttered toast fingers, mixed pickles and chutney are sometimes served with the fondue.

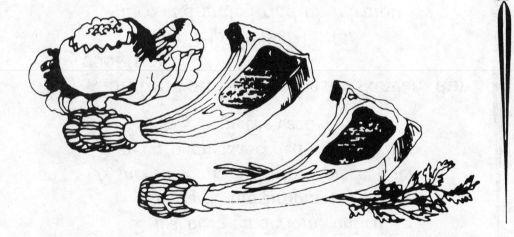

FONDUE ORIENTAL

Substitute lamb cubes, cut from leg of lamb, for beef and dip into a curry sauce made by beating 1 tbs curry powder into 1½ cups mayonnaise.

FRENCH FONDUE

Substitute boiling bouillon for the oil, and cut the meat—beef, veal, lamb, chicken, kidneys or liver—into slivers instead of pieces. Each guest spears two or three slivers at once, dips the meat into the simmering bouillon and dips the cooked meat into the same sauces as for Fondue Bourguignonne.

SKEWERED BEEF

(1) String alternately onto 6 skewers:
> 2 lbs beef tenderloin, cubed
> 12 large mushroom caps
> 6 slices bacon, cut into 3 pieces each
> 2 green peppers, seeded and cut into
> 6 pieces each

(2) Combine and use to baste skewers during cooking:
> ¾ cup melted butter
> juice and grated rind of 1 lemon
> 3 tbs chopped chives
> 1 tsp chopped rosemary
> salt and pepper to taste

(3) Broil 3 inches from heat, turning frequently and basting with above mixture. Broil approximately 12–15 minutes in all and serve with remaining butter mixture as a sauce.

STEAK AU POIVRE / PEPPER STEAK

Preheat oven to 200°F.

(1) Select Delmonico, shell, boned club steaks or filet mignon, weighing about 3 pounds in all:
> 6 boneless steaks, cut 1½ inches thick

(2) Crush with a mallet or back of wooden kitchen spoon in a wooden bowl or on a wooden board:
> 4 tbs black peppercorns,
> preferably Telicherry peppercorns

(3) Trim, wipe and dry steaks, season to taste with salt and pound the pepper into both sides of the steaks.

(4) Set plates and serving platter into the preheated oven.

(5) Set near stove a brush or cloth and bowl with:

3 tbs vegetable oil

(6) Oil heavy pans, set over high heat and when very hot, brush pans again with oil. Pan broil steaks according to timetable on page 10. Turn steaks only once. Transfer finished steaks to hot platter in oven.

(7) Add enough oil to one of the pans to make 1½ tbs. Add to pan and flame:
½ cup warmed brandy

(8) When flame dies down, add and boil, stirring, for just one minute, then pour sauce over steaks and serve immediately:
2 cups heavy cream
1 dash Kitchen Bouquet
2 tbs minced fresh herbs or parsley
and chives*

* If fresh herbs are available, mince together a sprig of parsley, a few tarragon and basil leaves, a sprig of thyme and a few spears of chives.

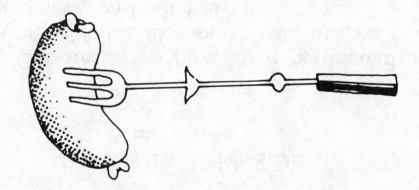

GARLIC STEAKS

(1) Combine and set aside for 12 hours:
  1 cup oil
  2 garlic cloves, peeled and split
  ½ tsp salt

(2) Dip into above oil and broil 5 minutes on each side as near heat as possible:
  6 1-inch-thick fillet steaks

(3) As soon as they are ready, salt to taste and grind pepper roughly over steaks.

Serve at once on hot plates with a watercress salad and small baked potatoes. Serve a red wine and a fruit dessert.

Increase cooking time 1–2 minutes on each side for medium rare, and longer if desired. The time given here is for rare steaks.

STEAK DIANE I

(1) Buy and have pounded to ½-inch thickness:
  1 1-inch-thick sirloin steak, about 2½ pounds

(2) Cut steak into pieces that correspond to your widest skillet and brown one at a time quickly on both sides in:
  6 tbs butter

(3) Roll up steak and push aside or set on hot platter and add to butter in skillet:
  5 shallots, chopped
  1 tbs Worcestershire sauce
  1 tbs Escoffier sauce
  2 tsp dry mustard
  salt and freshly ground black pepper to taste

(4) Return steak to pan and cook in sauce for 2–3 minutes, turning once, then add and flame:

5 tbs heated brandy

(5) Serve at once with the sauce in pan.

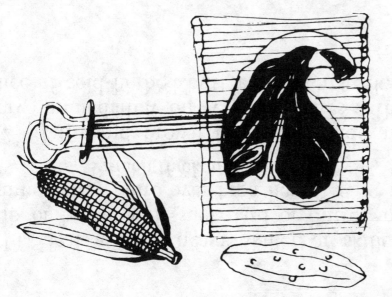

STEAK DIANE II

(1) Proceed as above for Steps 1 and 2. Substitute the following for Step 3:

2 tbs minced spring onions
2 tbs minced green pepper
1 tbs minced parsley
1 tbs Escoffier sauce
1 tbs Sauce Robert or Worcestershire sauce
3 tbs sour cream
salt and freshly ground black pepper to taste

(2) Proceed as above, but increase brandy to:

½ cup warmed brandy

MINUTE STEAKS

(1) Heat a large heavy skillet or skillets, rub or brush with suet, lard or butter and immediately sauté over high heat:

    6 ½-inch-thick minute steaks*

(2) Turn and brown the second side and serve immediately on very hot plates with a slice of cold herbed butter on each steak.

* Minute steaks can be ordered from any butcher. They are usually ½-inch-thick slices of top round, filet mignon, sirloin or club steak. Although called Minute Steaks, the sautéeing takes about 2 minutes in all. The meat should be brown on the outside, rare on the inside.

HERBED BUTTER

(1) Combine and chill:
    ½ cup soft butter
    1 minced shallot or spring onion
    1 tbs minced chives
    1 tbs minced parsley
    1 tbs minced tarragon
    1 tbs minced chervil

(2) Cut into portions and use with steaks.

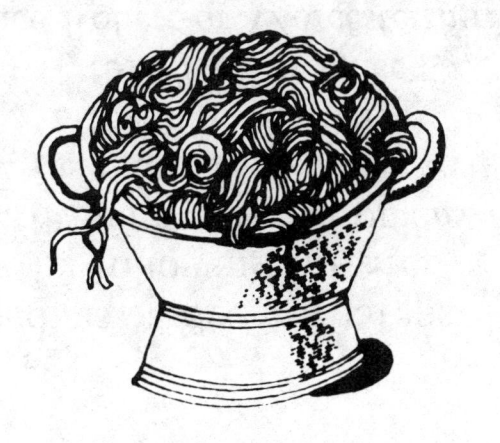

STEAKS WITH RED WINE SAUCE

Preheat oven to 200°F.

(1) Select club, rib or shell steaks weighing 3–3¾ lbs in all:

> 6 steaks, cut 1-inch thick

(2) Place plates and platter in preheated oven.

(3) Pan broil steaks, turning once, 8–10 minutes cooking time in all; transfer steaks to hot platter in oven and re-oil pans (see page 14 for basic Pan Broiling instructions).

(4.) Add to oil remaining in one of the pans and stir for 2 minutes:

> 2 tbs butter
> 2 shallots, minced

(5) Add and stir 1 minute longer:

> ¼ cup minced mushrooms

(6) Add and deglaze pan with:

> ½ cup red wine
> ½ cup strong beef bouillon

(7) Season sauce to taste with salt and freshly ground black pepper, pour over steaks and serve at once.

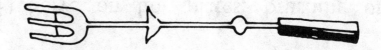

MARINATED STEAKS

(1) Combine and use as a marinade and for basting:

> 1 clove garlic, crushed with:
> ½ tsp salt
> 1 tbs dark brown sugar
> 1 cup sherry
> ½ cup soy sauce
> ¼ cup dry white wine
> salt and pepper to taste

(2) Trim club, Delmonico, shell or fillet steaks and place in marinade for 3–4 hours, turning frequently:

> 6 individual 1-inch-thick steaks

(3) Broil steaks, brushing with marinade, for 6–7 minutes on each side or to taste (see chart, page 9). Fillet steaks will take less time.

(4) Serve on hot plates, brushing once more with marinade just before serving.

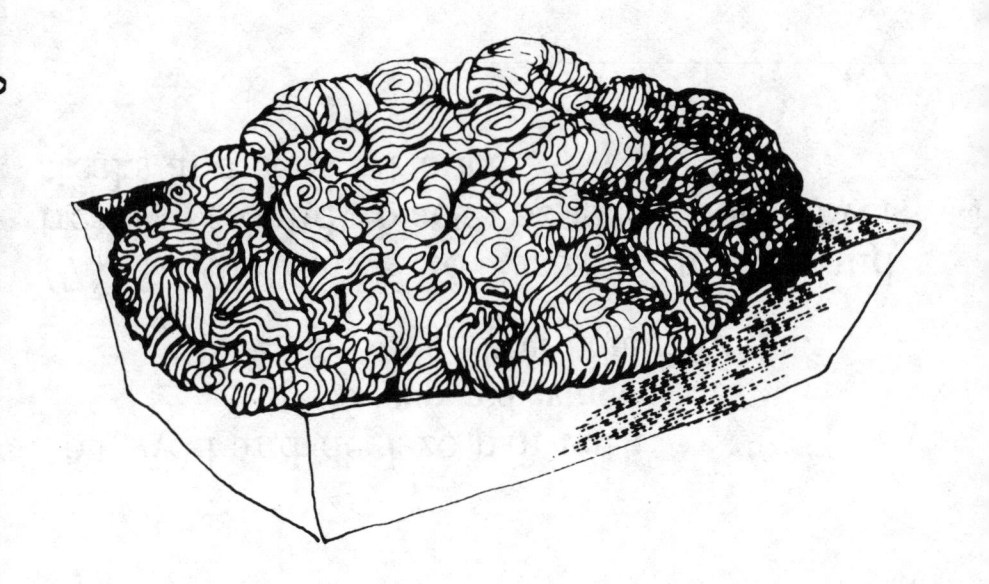

24

LONDON BROIL FLANK STEAK

(1) Broil on an oiled rack, about 3 inches from heat unit for 10 minutes, turning once after 5 minutes:

> 1 3-lb flank steak, marinated

(2) Season and transfer to a wooden board. Cover top with slices of:

> herbed butter, see page 22

(3) Slice steak on an angle, not with the grain, and serve immediately on warmed plates.

MARINADE FOR STEAK

(1) Combine and shake until dry ingredients are dissolved:

> 1 cup oil
> ½ cup vinegar
> 1 tbs lemon juice
> 1 tsp salt
> ½ tsp paprika
> ½ tsp dry mustard
> ¼ tsp pepper
> 1 clove garlic, crushed

FILETS MIGNONS

This is an expensive cut, for gala occasions. Most butchers will prepare 1- to 1½-inch-thick slices with a piece of fat pork tied around the meat. These make individual servings, and can be pan broiled in 6–14 minutes, depending on thickness.

Filets mignons are enhanced by garnishes and sauces. Some are classics, others are inventions, but the fact remains that there is no point in spending excessive time on the sauces and garnishes when the meat itself takes less than 15 minutes to prepare. The following recipes are suggestions for sauces, garnishes and accompaniments that can be made while the steaks are broiling.

BEEF FILLET STROGANOFF

(1) Cut meat into strips as long and thick as your little finger, and dredge well in the flour:

1½ lbs fillet of beef
salted flour for dredging

(2) Brown the dredged meat well on all sides in:

3 tbs butter

(3) Add to pan and cook 3 minutes longer:

2 cups sliced mushrooms
1 medium onion, sliced very fine
1 small clove garlic, crushed

(4) Remove meat, mushrooms and onion from pan with a slotted spoon and keep warm. Add to pan:

3 tbs butter

(5) Stir into pan gradually:

3 tbs flour
1½ tbs tomato paste

(6) Add to pan and stir until smooth:

½ sour pickle, finely diced and drained
1½ cups cold beef broth

(7) Return meat, onion and mushrooms to pan, let liquid boil up once, reduce heat, add and heat through but do not boil again:

1½ cups sour cream
3 tbs sherry

(8) Serve with noodles or rice and pass a pepper mill separately.

FILET MIGNON WITH SAUCES AND ACCOMPANIMENTS

(1) Lightly flatten steaks with heel of hand and dip in butter:

> 6 1-inch-thick fillet steaks
> ½ cup melted butter

(2) Broil on oiled rack according to directions on page 9.

(3) Serve at once on very hot plates on:

> ½-inch-thick bread rounds fried in
> butter until golden
> Slices of canned goose liver pâté

SERVE WITH:

(1) Crisp watercress
(2) Heated and crisped shoestring potatoes
(3) Heated and crisp potato chips
(4) Broiled onion slices
(5) Broiled mushrooms
(6) Broiled tomatoes
(7) Strips of fried or broiled bacon

SERVE WITH ANY OF THESE SAUCES:

(1) Béarnaise Sauce, see page 31
(2) Tyrolean Sauce I or II, see page 31
(3) Mushroom sauce
(4) Tomato sauce
(5) Hot sauce, see page 40

CORNED BEEF HASH UNDER CHEESE

(1) Split with a fork and toast lightly on split side:

> 6 English muffins

(2) Butter muffins lightly and set aside:

> 4 tbs butter

(3) Combine and stir over low heat until heated through:

> 1 1-lb can corned beef hash
> 1 small onion, chopped
> ½ cup sliced stuffed olives
> 1 dill pickle, chopped and drained
> ½ cup tomato catsup
> salt and pepper to taste

(4) Divide hash mixture on the muffin halves and top with:

> 12 slices sharp cheese

(5) Arrange muffins on broiler rack and broil only long enough to melt and brown the cheese.

(6) Serve hot with additional catsup and pickles.

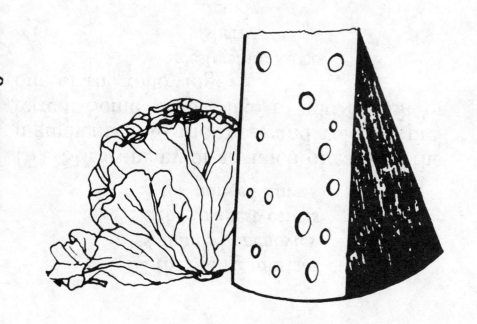

BEEFSTEAK TARTARE

(1) With a strong silver spoon, scrape:

> 3 lbs top round of beef,
> cut in one thick piece

(2) Gather the meat as it is collected in the spoon onto a dish and cover until all meat is scraped and only gristle and fat remain.

(3) Shape meat into two balls on a wooden serving platter or board and make a depression in the center of each. Drop into the depressions:

> 2 unbroken raw egg yolks

(4) Surround the meat with little mounds of the following:

> 2 tsp salt
> 1 tsp pepper
> 2 tsp paprika
> finely chopped onion
> finely chopped dill pickle

> 2 tbs brown mustard
> 4 minced anchovies
> 2 tbs smallest capers
> 2 tbs minced chives

(5) Stir as many or as much of each of the ingredients into the meat and yolks as preferred. Some people like to add a dash of one of the following:

> Worcestershire sauce
> sherry
> brandy
> tomato catsup

(6) Serve the mixed raw beef with slices of buttered black or rye bread.

(7) It is customary to ask whether any guests want to omit any of the ingredients, in which case they are served before the addition of that ingredient.

BÉARNAISE SAUCE

(1) Boil down to reduce liquid to 2 tbs, cool and strain:

> 1 tbs chopped shallots
> 1 pinch white pepper
> 1 pinch salt
> 1 tbs fresh minced tarragon leaves
> ½ cup wine vinegar

(2) In the top of a double boiler, over— not touching—simmering water, beat:

> 3 egg yolks

(3) Gradually beat in, one piece at a time:

> 12 tbs cold butter, cut into 12 pieces

(4) Add reduced mixture from Step 1, alternating with above butter pieces.

(5) When sauce is thick and light, stir in and serve at once:

> 1 tbs minced tarragon leaves
> 1 tbs minced chervil leaves

If dried herbs are used, reduce their quantity in Steps 1 and 5 to half.

TYROLEAN SAUCE I

Prepare as for a mayonnaise, ¾ cup oil beaten into 3 egg yolks, using the reduced essence from Step 1 of the Béarnaise Sauce instead of vinegar. Add minced herbs as in Béarnaise Sauce.

TYROLEAN SAUCE II

Prepare Tyrolean Sauce I, adding a drop of red vegetable coloring and 3 tbs tomato puree just before serving.

BROILED TOMATOES

(1) Cut in half across:
    3 large tomatoes

(2) Brush cut surfaces with:
    2 tbs melted butter

(3) Sprinkle with:
    1 tbs minced onion
    1 tbs minced parsley
    salt and pepper to taste

(4) Place, cut side up, under broiler at low heat and broil gently to soften tomatoes without scorching, about 6 minutes.

(5) Just before serving, the tomatoes may be sprinkled with cheese and broiled rapidly until brown, about 2 minutes.

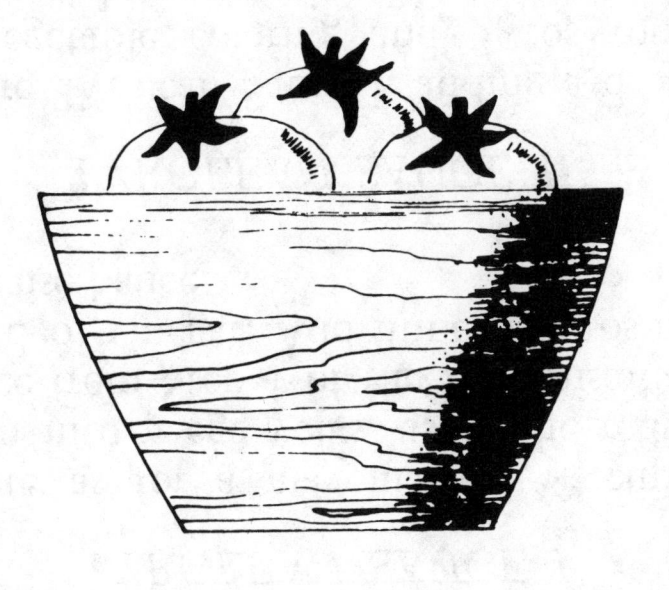

VARIATIONS:

(I) Sprinkle with a mixture of bread crumbs, cheese and parsley.

(II) Sprinkle with chopped ripe olives and bread crumbs.

(III) Sprinkle with thyme, oregano and seasonings.

GRILLED MUSHROOMS

(1) Combine on waxed paper, shape into a narrow oblong and chill, then slice into 24 or 36 pieces:

⅔ cup butter, creamed
2 cloves garlic, crushed
1 tbs minced parsley
2 tbs onion
salt and pepper to taste

(2) Clean with a soft cloth, break out stems* and place hollow-side down on an oiled grill or ovenware dish:

24 large or 36 medium mushrooms

(3) Brush lightly with oil and broil 3 minutes.

(4) Turn mushrooms, fill cavity with above butter slices and broil until sizzling and tender, about 5 minutes for medium and 8 minutes for large mushrooms.

Serve with broiled steaks or broiled chicken.

* Save the mushroom stems to use in a sauce or soup.

BROILED ONION SLICES

(1) Cut large yellow onions into slices as· thick as your little finger.

(2) Place on an oiled grill and sprinkle generously with paprika.

(3) Broil 2 minutes on top broiler shelf, or as close to heat as possible.

(4) Salt and pepper to taste and serve with broiled steaks, hamburgers, lamb chops or broiled fish.

BROILED ONION SLICES ON TOMATO SLICES

(1) Cut onions and tomatoes across into ⅓-inch slices.

(2) Brush generously with oil and salt and pepper.

(3) Broil on an oiled grill as close to heat as possible for 2 minutes, turn with a spatula and broil 1 minute longer.

(4) Place each onion slice on a tomato slice and sprinkle with paprika and chopped parsley.

Serve with any broiled meat or fish.

FRITTERS / AN ACCOMPANIMENT

In a deep fat fryer or heavy pot

Heat deep fat to 390°F on a deep-fat thermometer.

(1) Beat in a bowl until smooth and set aside for 1 hour:

    ½ cup flour
    ½ tsp salt
    1 egg yolk
    1 tbs melted butter
    ½ cup beer

(2) Fold in:

    2 egg whites, stiffly beaten

(3) Dip into batter, fry in deep fat and serve on a napkin with lemon slices and tartar sauce:

artichoke hearts
cauliflower flowerets
asparagus spears
mushrooms
banana sections
apple slices
peach halves
or anything that sounds good

ONIONS FOR SMOTHERING

(1) Lightly brown in butter in a heavy pan on top of stove:

> 6 medium onions, sliced very thin
> 3 tbs butter

(2) Transfer to broiler pan and place below steak or liver. Let drippings from meat fall over onions.

(3) Season with:

> salt and pepper to taste

(4) Serve steak or liver topped with the onions.

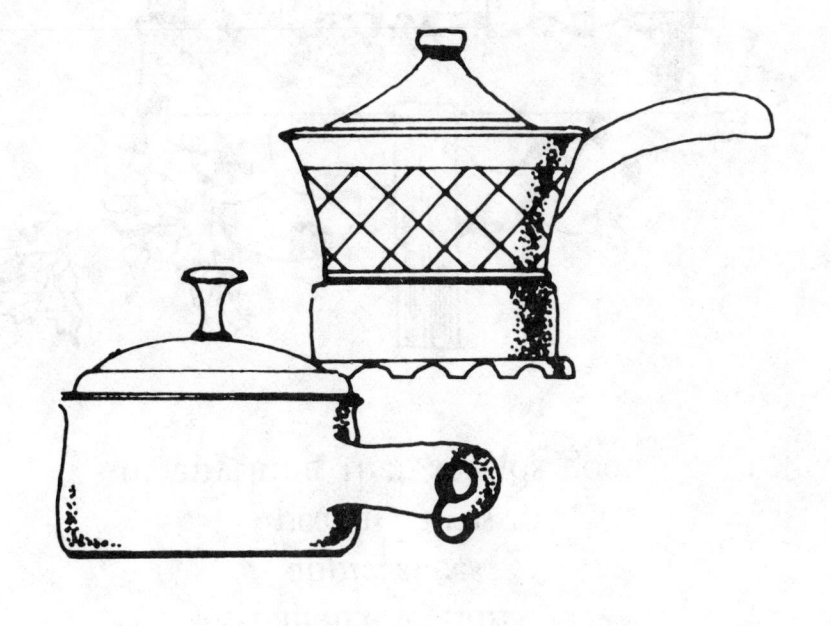

HAMBURGERS AND FRANKFURTERS

GROUND MEAT FOR HAMBURGERS

(1) Ready-ground hamburger is economical and good for most purposes. It comes in two varieties: *Regular*, which may not contain more than 25% fat and *Lean*, which may not contain more than 12% fat. Both varieties are ground twice.

(2) Freshly ground, to order, hamburger is a matter of taste. *Chuck* is juicier than *round*. Always ask the butcher to grind the meat—once for juicy hamburgers, twice for regular purposes and three times for small meat balls, meat loaf and cocktail hamburgers.

(3) About 2½ lbs of hamburger make a generous serving for 6 people. When other ingredients are added, the amount of meat can be reduced accordingly.

PAN BROILED HAMBURGER STEAKS

(1) Shape into 6 large balls, flatten slightly and brown on both sides with the bacon:

2½ lbs ground beef
3 slices bacon, diced while cold

(2) Add, reduce heat and cook, covered, while preparing sauce:

1 green pepper, seeded and diced

(3) Brown onion in butter, stir in flour until smooth, add remaining ingredients and stir until thickened:

3 onions, chopped
4 tbs butter
4 tbs flour
¾ cup bouillon
½ cup red wine, or to taste
½ cup thick tomato sauce
salt and pepper to taste

(4) Pour sauce over hamburgers and simmer a few minutes longer. Serve, sprinkled with:

¼ cup chopped parsley

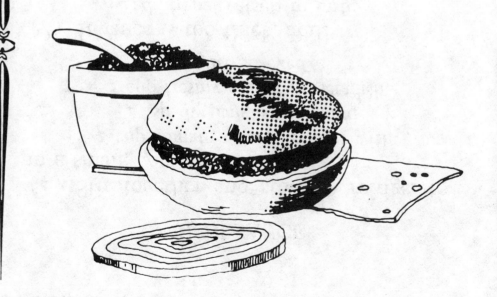

INFRA-RED BROILED HAMBURGERS WITH HOT SAUCE

(1) Shape into 6 thick loaflike ovals:
>   *2½ lbs ground chuck*

(2) Sprinkle tops with:
>   *garlic salt to taste*
>   *Dash or any seasoned salt, to taste*

(3) Place on top rack as near heat unit as possible and broil 6 minutes on each side for rare; increase time to taste for medium or well done.

(4) Remove with pancake turner and serve at once on hot plates with:
>   *1 cup hot sauce*

HOT SAUCE

(1) Stir together and store in refrigerator in a small, covered crock:
>   *½ cup tomato catsup, stirred with:*
>   *2 tsp dry English mustard*
>   *½ cup freshly grated horseradish, tightly packed*

(2) If sauce is too thick, add:
>   *additional catsup to taste*

SHISH KABOB HAMBURGERS

(1) Combine, mix well and shape into 18 balls:

$1\frac{1}{2}$ lbs ground beef
$\frac{1}{4}$ lb ground pork
1 large egg
$\frac{1}{2}$ cup cracker meal
2 tbs bread crumbs
$\frac{3}{4}$ cup evaporated milk
1 medium onion, chopped
1 tbs brown mustard
$\frac{1}{2}$ clove garlic, crushed
salt and pepper to taste

(2) Divide equally and string on 6 skewers, alternating ingredients on the skewers:

the hamburger balls
18 small tomatoes
18 mushroom caps
12 small onions, quartered

(3) Place the filled skewers across a broiler pan and brush with:

$\frac{1}{4}$ cup melted butter

(4) Broil 5 inches from heat for 5 minutes on each side. Season and serve with rice:

salt and pepper to taste

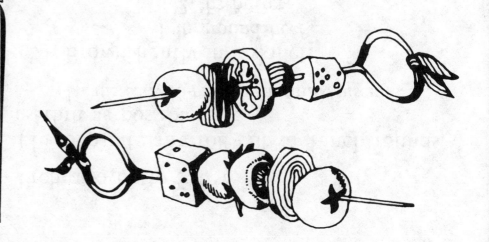

HAMBURGERS WITH CHILI SAUCE

(1) Pan fry or broil until done to taste, 4–8 minutes a side:
1½ lbs ground chuck, shaped into 6 patties

(2) While the hamburgers are cooking, toast:
6 hamburger rolls, split

(3) Heat together until hot:
1 1-lb can chili con carne
¼ cup red wine or bouillon

(4) Place hamburgers on rolls, pour over the heated chili, cover tops with cheese slices and brown under broiler until cheese melts and starts to brown:
½ roll garlic-smoked cheese,
cut into thin slices

HAMBURGER PIZZAS

Preheat oven to 550°F.

(1) Separate and roll out to 4-inch rounds, as thin as possible:
1 can ready-to-bake buttermilk biscuits

(2) Brown lightly in a skillet:
1 lb ground beef
2 tbs butter

(3) Divide the browned meat over the biscuit rounds and divide over the meat:
1 jar tomato spaghetti sauce
1 small can sliced mushrooms
2 tsp dried oregano
12 slices mozzarella cheese
¼ cup grated Parmesan cheese

(4) Bake in hot oven for about 10 minutes, or until cheese has melted and edges of biscuits are browned. Serve at once.

(1) Combine, mix well and shape into small bullets:

> 2 lbs lean ground beef
> 1 egg
> ¾ cup milk
> 2 tbs grated onion
> ½ tsp dried thyme
> ½ tsp dried marjoram
> salt and pepper to taste

(2) Roll bullets in:

> ¼ cup paprika

(3) Place on a sheet of aluminum foil on top broiler rack and broil or pan fry until browned on the outside and pink inside. Shake rack or pan to turn the bullets frequently and broil only 2–3 minutes in all.

(4) Combine with:

> 1 recipe Barbecue Sauce, page 44

> or 1 jar spaghetti sauce

(5) Serve with wooden picks as a cocktail appetizer or pour over freshly cooked spaghetti and serve at once with grated Parmesan cheese.

HAMBURG BULLETS II

(1) Sauté for 4 minutes and drain well:
3 medium onions, finely chopped
2 tbs oil

(2) Combine, mix well and shape into small bullets:
2 lbs lean ground beef
the sautéed and drained onions
2 eggs
2 jiggers brandy

(3) Dredge bullets with:
¼ cup paprika

(4) Broil or pan fry as for Hamburg Bullets I. Serve with Barbecue Sauce.

BARBECUE SAUCE

(1) Brown lightly in a wide pan for about 4 minutes:
3 tbs chopped onion
2 tbs oil

(2) Add and simmer 12 minutes:
1½ cups chili sauce
½ cup catsup
2 tbs brown mustard
2 tsp Worcestershire sauce
¼ cup brown sugar
1 tsp dried oregano
½ tsp ground allspice

(3) Pour sauce over Hamburg Bullets and serve as cocktail appetizer.

FILLED HAMBURGERS

(1) Combine in a large bowl and mix together well:

2½ lbs ground chuck
½ cup pretzel crumbs
½ cup seasoned bread crumbs
scant ½ cup soy sauce
¾ cup finely minced onion
3 small shallots or green onions, minced
pepper to taste
¼ cup chopped parsley

(2) Divide into 12 equal portions and shape into balls. Flatten half the balls and divide over them:

12 thin mushroom slices
12 pitted black olives, sliced

(3) Flatten remaining balls and cover over filled halves. Seal edges together very well.

(4) Combine and brush over the filled hamburgers:

4 tbs black olive juice, from can or jar
2 tbs soy sauce
½ tsp Worcestershire sauce
½ tsp sugar

(5) Grill, broil or pan fry hamburgers, brushing often with the marinade, until browned on the outside and done to taste, 4–6 minutes on each side.

VARIATIONS ON FILLINGS:

(I) Fill hamburgers with 1 tbs shredded lettuce each.

(II) Fill hamburgers with 1 tbs grated sharp cheese each.

(III) Fill hamburgers with a small round of thin tomato slices.

(1) Shape meat around the stuffed olives with floured hands. Make hamburgers just large enough to cover olives well:

1 lb ground chuck
1 jar smallest stuffed olives
¼ cup flour

(2) Roll hamburgers in:

¼ cup paprika

(3) Fry in heavy pan, shaking to fry until browned all over, in:

3 tbs butter

(4) As soon as hamburgers are well browned, season to taste and serve hot on cocktail picks:

salt and pepper to taste

VARIATIONS:

Vary stuffing by using a small cube of Bleu cheese or Roquefort cheese the same size as the small olives, or stuff with a small chunk of ice. If ice is used, fry at once before it melts. The ice leaves a very juicy center in the hamburger.

SWEDISH MEAT BALLS

(1) Have butcher grind together twice:
> 1 lb ground beef
> ½ lb ground veal
> ½ lb ground lean pork

(2) Fry until lightly browned:
> 1 onion, minced
> 2 tbs butter

(3) In a bowl, add to ground meat and beat until well mixed:
> 1 egg, beaten
> ½ cup bread crumbs
> the browned minced onion
> ½ cup milk
> salt and pepper to taste

(4) Shape into small balls with floured hands and fry in butter until browned, shaking pan to brown evenly:
> ¼ cup butter
> 3 tbs oil

(5) Keep meat balls hot in a heated, covered casserole. To juices left in pan, add and boil 1 minute, stirring constantly, then pour over meat balls and serve:
> ½ cup strong bouillon
> 1 cup heavy cream
> salt and pepper to taste

ENGLISH BEEF AND SAUSAGE CAKES

(1) Stir together until well blended:
> *1 lb ground beef*
> *1 lb sausage meat*

(2) Shape meat into 12 round, thin cakes. Divide over half the cakes, cover with the remaining cakes and press together well so that the apple slices are completely enclosed:
> *1 large sweet apple, peeled,*
> *cored and sliced very thin*

(3) Brown cakes quickly on both sides in:
> *3 tbs butter*

(4) Reduce heat and cook, covered, until apples are tender, about 15 minutes.

(5) Serve at once on hot plates with pan juices deglazed with:
> *1 cup boiling bouillon*
> *1 tbs brandy*

ENGLISH BEEF CAKES

Preheat oven to 200°F.

(1) Stir together until well blended:
> 2 lbs ground beef
> 2 egg yolks, beaten
> salt and pepper to taste

(2) Divide meat into 6 portions, press into the center of each and flatten into patties:
> 2 tbs grated horseradish*

(3) Fry beef cakes in a heavy pan, until well browned on both sides but still pink inside, in:

> 3 tbs butter

(4) Set browned cakes on a platter in the oven. Add to butter remaining in pan and boil for 1 minute, stirring:
> 1 cup heavy cream
> 1 tbs French mustard, stirred with:

> 1 tbs warm water
> salt and pepper to taste

(5) Pour sauce over beef cakes and serve at once.

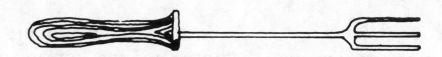

* If bottled horseradish is used, drain it well.

FRANKFURTERS

Frankfurters can be purchased "skinless" or with natural skin or casing. There are all-meat frankfurters, and all-beef frankfurters and most of them come in 3 sizes:

Regular, about 10 to a pound
Large, about 5 to a pound
Cocktail, about 27 to a pound

Frankfurters are usually packaged in ½-pound and 1-pound packages, in 2-pound or larger cartons, or in cans and glass jars. They can be kept for several days in the refrigerator, or for about a week in the freezer. If they are to be frozen for longer than a week, wrap and seal them in freezer paper.

Frankfurters are ready-cooked and can be eaten cold.

If they are to be heated, place in simmering water for about 7 minutes. They split open when put in boiling water. Take out with tongs or spoons; do not pierce the skin with a fork.

Frankfurters broil for about 5 minutes on each side, 5 inches from the heat unit. Brush with oil or rub with butter before broiling.

Frankfurters are pan broiled either whole or split. If split, start cooking with split-side down. Turn the frankfurters frequently, and cook until glossy and lightly browned.

In Germany, frankfurters are usually called Wienerwürste—Viennese sausages.

FRANKFURTER SANDWICHES I

(1) Split in half, but do not cut all the way through:

> 6 large frankfurters

(2) Fill with:

> 6 long, narrow slices sharp cheese

(3) Close frankfurters, wrap around them securely and fasten with picks:

> 6 slices bacon

(4) Push under broiler and broil, turning several times until bacon is crisp and brown. Drain and serve with:

> mustard

FRANKFURTER SANDWICHES II

Prepare frankfurters as above, but fill with well-drained crushed pineapple. Wrap in bacon and broil as above.

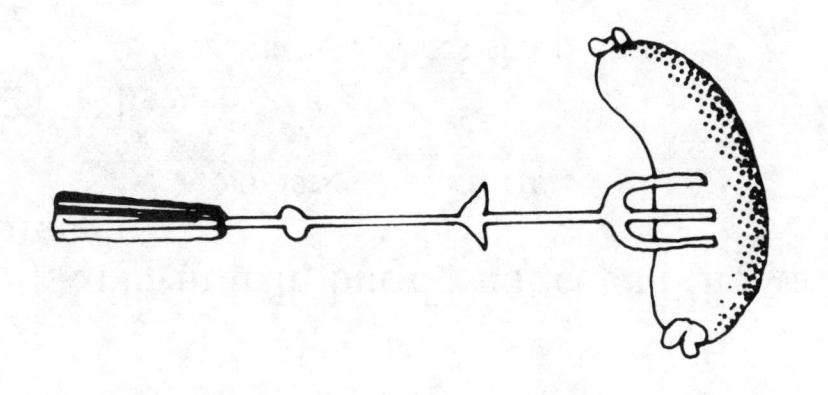

FRANKFURTER SANDWICHES III

Prepare frankfurters as above, but fill with mustard and sweet pickle relish. Wrap in bacon and broil as above.

COCKTAIL FRANKFURTER ROUNDS

Preheat oven to 325°F.

(1) Spread bread with mixture of remaining ingredients:

6 slices soft white bread, crusts removed
5 tbs soft cream cheese, mixed with:
1 tbs sharp mustard

(2) Place on prepared bread slices, roll up and secure with picks:

6 skinless frankfurters

(3) Brush bread rolls with:

3 tbs melted butter

(4) Bake 10–12 minutes, or until lightly browned. Cut into ½-inch slices, remove picks and serve.

BROILED FRANKFURTER MUFFINS

(1) Split with a fork, place on broiler rack and toast lightly:

    3 English muffins

(2) Spread hot muffins with:

    2 tbs soft butter

(3) Cover with large slices of:

    3 tomatoes, peeled
    salt and pepper to taste

(4) Top tomato slices with:

    6 frankfurters, split and halved
    6 square slices soft yellow cheese

(5) Push under broiler and broil until cheese melts and browns lightly at the edges.

FRANKFURTERS AND SAUERKRAUT

(1) Simmer in a saucepan over medium heat for 1½ hours, stirring often:

    1 1-lb 13-ounce can sauerkraut, undrained
    2 tsp caraway seeds

(2) Sprinkle over sauerkraut and stir until lightly thickened:

    2 tbs flour

(3) Add and stir well:

    1 1-lb can sliced apples

(4) Spread over sauerkraut and simmer 12 minutes:

    6 frankfurters, split in half

(5) Add:

    1 cup sour cream, beaten with:
    1 tsp paprika and
    1 tbs brown mustard
    salt and pepper to taste

(6) Do not stir until serving.

THICK BLACK BEAN SOUP

(1) Heat together to just under boiling:
   3 cans black bean soup
   9 skinless frankfurters, sliced thin

(2) Take from heat, stir in and pour into bowls or soup plates:
   ½ cup sherry

(3) Divide over portions:
   6 hard-cooked eggs, sliced

(4) Serve at once as a meal-in-itself soup.

FRANKFURTER GREEN PEA SOUP

(1) Prepare according to label instructions:
   3 cans smoky green pea soup

(2) Add and cook until heated through:
   8 skinless frankfurters, sliced thin

(3) Add just before serving:
   ¼ cup sherry

(4) Serve in bowls or soup plates, covered with:
   2 hard-cooked eggs, riced
   2 tbs chopped parsley

Preheat oven to 200°F.

(1) Have butcher cut a 4–5-inch diameter bologna sausage into slices, leaving the skin on. Any slice with a broken skin will not curl when fried. In a wide, heavy pan, fry until they curl into cups, remove and keep warm in oven:

> 6 slices bologna sausage, 1/5-inch thick
> 1 tbs fat or butter

(2) To pan, add butter, beat eggs with remaining ingredients and scramble to taste:

> 1 tbs butter
> 6 eggs
> 1 tbs minced chives or onion
> 1 tbs water
> 2 tbs cream
> ¼ tsp salt
> freshly ground black pepper to taste

(3) Fill eggs into bologna cups, sprinkle over and serve hot:

> 1 tsp paprika

VARIATION: Place on top of each egg-filled bologna cup and push under broiler until browned:

> 6 thin slices Cheddar cheese

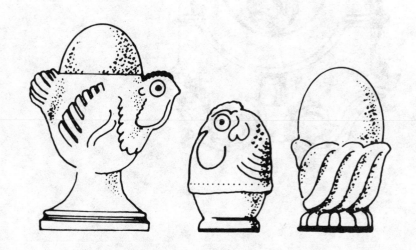

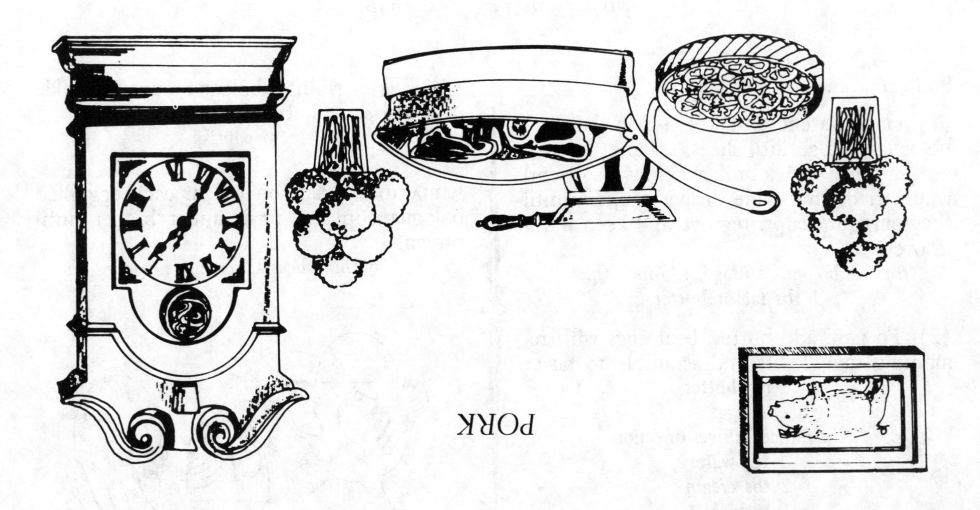

PORK

HAM STEAKS STANLEY

Preheat oven to 375°F.

(1) Broil for about 4 minutes on each side:
6 ham steaks, about 8 ounces each

(2) Cut lengthwise, set in a buttered pan, sprinkle with sugar and bake 5–7 minutes, or until soft and browned:
6 large bananas

Serve ham steaks on hot plates with 2 banana halves on each. Accompany with mashed potatoes and horseradish sauce.

HORSERADISH SAUCE

(1) Peel and grate:
1 small horseradish root

(2) Stir in a saucepan and boil for 2 minutes:

the grated horseradish
1 cup bread crumbs
heavy cream to cover
salt and pepper to taste
1 pinch sugar

BAKED HAM AND SOUR CHERRY SAUCE

Preheat oven to 375°F.

(1) Heat in a double boiler over boiling water until jelly is melted:

> 1 jar whole sour cherry preserves
> 1 orange, juice and grated rind
> ½ tsp ground cloves
> ½ tsp ground ginger
> ½ tsp dry mustard

(2) Arrange in a buttered baking dish, pour over the sauce and bake until sizzling, about 15 minutes:

> 6 ready-to-eat cooked ham slices,
> cut ¼ inch thick

HAM STEAKS WITH PINEAPPLE

(1) Combine and mix together well:

> 1 cup brown sugar
> 1 cup dry white wine
> pineapple juice drained from
> 1   1-lb 4-ounce can pineapple chunks
> 1 tbs brown mustard
> salt and pepper to taste

(2) Trim, dry and marinate in above mixture for 30 minutes:

> 3 ½-inch-thick ready-to-eat ham steaks

(3) Remove ham from marinade and broil 1 minute. Spread over ham:

> 3 tsp brown mustard

(4) To marinade, add and heat to boiling:

> the pineapple chunks

(5) Continue to broil ham until sizzling, then serve on hot plates with the hot pineapple sauce poured over.

58

HAM WITH RAISINS

(1) Brown quickly on both sides in 2 heavy pans with no additional fat:

   6 precooked ham slices, ½ inch thick

(2) Combine and pour over ham slices, dividing equally between the pans:

   1½ cups red wine
   ½ jar apple jelly
   ⅓ cup dark raisins

(3) Let the sauce boil until it is almost evaporated and begins to wrap itself around the ham. Turn the slices occasionally.

(4) Serve immediately with the remaining sauce—which should be quite thick—poured over.

HAM IN SPICE SAUCE

Preheat oven to 375°F.

(1) Arrange in a wide baking pan in a single layer:

   6 ¼-inch-thick ready-to-eat ham slices

(2) Melt in top of double boiler over boiling water, stir well, pour over ham slices and bake until ham is heated through:

   1 jar red currant jelly
   2 tbs vinegar
   ½ tsp cinnamon
   ½ tsp ground cloves
   ½ tsp dry mustard

(3) Serve at once.

HAM WITH ORANGE SAUCE

(1) Brown quickly with no additional fat in two heavy pans:

> 6 cooked ham slices, ½ inch thick

(2) Combine and pour over ham, dividing equally between the pans:

> 1½ cups orange juice
> ½ cup loosely packed brown sugar
> 3 tbs grated orange rind
> 2 tbs honey

(3) Let the sauce boil until it is almost evaporated and begins to wrap itself around the ham slices.

(4) Serve immediately with the remaining sauce—which should be quite thick—poured over.

(5) Garnish each ham slice with a thin slice of orange with the peel removed.

BAKED HAM CASSEROLE

Preheat oven to 400°F.

(1) Arrange in a 1½-quart buttered casserole with ham slices standing upright in a circle:

> 1 1½-lb canned Danish ham,
>   cut in thick slices
> 1 1½-lb can sweet potatoes
> 1 can sliced pineapple

(2) Combine and pour over casserole:

> juice from ham can
> juice from canned pineapple
> ½ tsp brown mustard
> ¼ tsp cinnamon
> ¼ tsp ground ginger
> ¼ tsp ground cloves

(3) Sprinkle over and bake until sizzling and browned:

> ⅓ cup tightly packed brown sugar

PORK AND GREEN PEPPERS

(1) Mix until smooth with enough water to make a paste:

> 2 tbs flour
> ¼ cup soy sauce
> 2 tbs brown sugar

(2) Fry for 4 minutes in a heavy pan:

> 2 tbs lard
> 6 spring onions, chopped
> 1 clove garlic, crushed

(3) Add and fry for 5 minutes longer:

> 4 green peppers, seeded and diced

(4) Add and fry until browned:

> 3 lbs pork loin, cut into thin, short strips
> salt and pepper to taste

(5) Add soy sauce mixture from Step 1 and simmer 4 minutes longer. Serve at once.

DICED PORK AND PEANUTS

(1) Brown in a hot pan:

> 1½ lbs diced raw lean pork
> 3 tbs oil

(2) Add and stir well for 3 minutes:

> 3 tbs soy sauce

(3) Add and cook, covered, for 3 minutes:

> 3 large carrots, scraped and finely diced

(4) Add and cook, covered, for 4 minutes:

> 3 large green peppers, seeded and diced
> 1 cup peanuts

(5) Add, stir well and serve very hot as soon as sugar is absorbed:

> 3 tbs brown sugar

Serve with rice.

PORK WITH BROCCOLI

(1) Combine and set aside:
    2 tbs soy sauce
    ½ tsp shredded ginger
    2 tsp sugar
    1 tsp saki or sherry
    1 tbs water

(2) Combine and set aside:
    ½ cup water
    1½ tbs cornstarch
    1 tsp soy sauce
    1 pinch pepper
    1 tsp MSG

(3) Boil uncovered for about 4 minutes, then drain:
    2 bunches broccoli, washed and cut into
    1-inch lengths

(4) In a heavy pan, heat:
    2 tbs peanut oil
    ½ tsp salt

(5) Add and stir each ingredient well before adding the next. Fry, stirring, for 5 minutes or until browned:
    1 clove garlic, crushed
    ½ lb raw pork tenderloin or butt,
    sliced very thin
    soy sauce mixture, Step 1
    broccoli, Step 3
    ½ cup thinly sliced celery
    ½ cup thinly sliced onion
    2 tbs French or Chinese mushrooms,
    sliced thin

(6) Add and cook, covered, for 2 minutes:
    1 cup stock

(7) Add mixture from Step 2 and stir until thickened. Serve at once.

SPARERIBS

(1) Combine in a very large bowl and mix together well:

    2 cups soy sauce
    1 cup pineapple juice
    ⅔ cup sherry
    4 tbs brown sugar
    ½ tsp ground ginger
    ½ tsp ground cloves
    2 cloves garlic, crushed

(2) Add and marinate 6–8 hours, turning frequently:

    3 sides of spareribs, cut into single ribs

(3) Remove spareribs from marinade, arrange on a broiler rack about 1 inch from the flame or heat unit and broil 7 minutes, basting constantly. Turn ribs and broil second side, basting constantly, for about 5 minutes.

(4) Serve as a main course with rice, or serve these ribs to 12 people as a cocktail party appetizer with paper napkins or with cuffs on the bone end to facilitate eating.

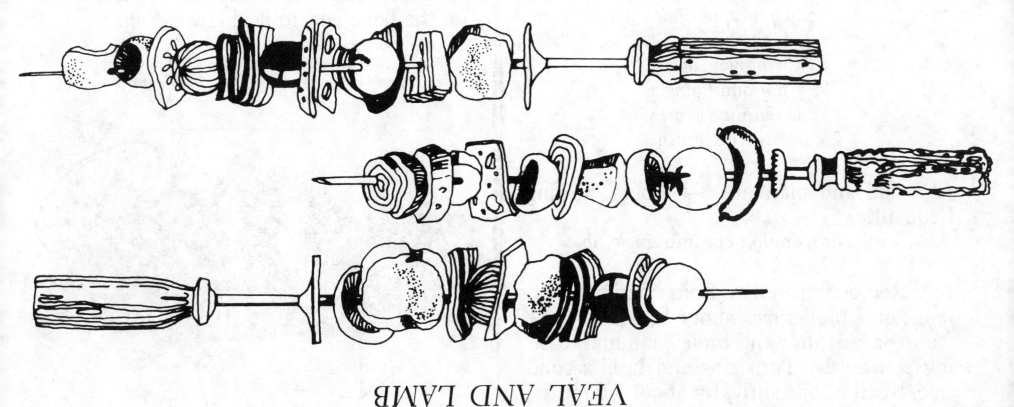

VEAL AND LAMB

VEAL CUTLETS SCALLOPINI / SCHNITZEL

The veal cutlet is a slice of meat cut from across the leg of veal. It is similar to the ham steak. It is usually cut thin, about ⅜ to ½ inch thick, and pounded to about 1/5-inch thickness. It can be bought already pounded and cut for scallopini, or the butcher will pound it on request. Allow 4–5 ounces boneless veal per person.

If you have to pound the veal:

Slice the cutlets into serving pieces—it falls into natural divisions—and discard any bone or gristle. Place veal, one piece at a time, between two layers of heavy butcher's paper or waxed paper. Pound gently with a wooden mallet until the surface of the cutlet has increased and the desired thickness is reached—about 1/5 inch or less. Pound evenly so that the edges do not become too thin. The pounded cutlets can be refrigerated with a piece of waxed paper between each cutlet.

Use pounded veal cutlets for the following recipes.

VEAL SCALLOPINI MARSALA

(1) Melt butter in a wide pan over medium heat. Add dredged meat and sauté until lightly browned, turning once, then set aside and keep warm:

> 4 tbs butter
> 2 lbs veal, prepared for scallopini,
> dredged in:
> ¼ cup seasoned flour

(2) Add to pan and scrape in all pan juices, then simmer 3 minutes:

> ⅔ cup dry Marsala wine
> ⅓ cup strong beef stock or
> ⅓ cup water and 1 beef bouillon cube
> salt and pepper to taste

(3) Return meat to pan, simmer for 1 minute and serve on hot plates.

The quantity of meat can be reduced to 1½ lbs when scallopini are served with pasta or rice.

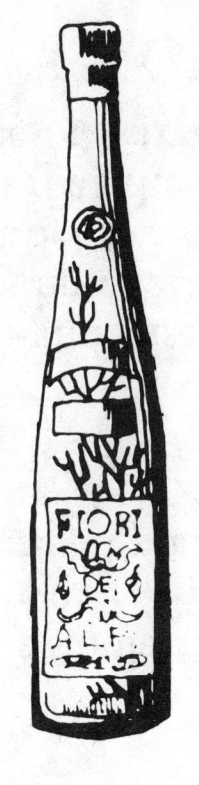

VEAL SCALLOPINI WITH TONGUE

(1) Dredge veal in seasoned flour, dip in milk and again in flour:

> 1½ lbs veal scallopini,
> pounded and cut into pieces
> seasoned flour for dredging
> ⅔ cup milk

(2) Cook veal quickly until golden on both sides in:

> 4 tbs butter

(3) Remove veal and keep warm. Add to pan:

> 4 tbs chopped onion
> 1 clove garlic, split
> ½ cup Marsala wine
> 1 tbs chopped parsley

(4) Discard garlic, return veal to pan, add and simmer 3 minutes:

> ½ cup slivered cooked beef tongue
> ¼ cup bouillon

(5) Serve immediately on warmed plates.

VEAL SCALLOPINI WITH MARSALA

(1) Sauté veal in butter until golden on both sides and transfer veal to a hot platter and keep warm:

1½ pounds veal cutlets, pounded thin, cut into serving pieces and dredged in:
seasoned flour
4 tbs butter

(2) Add to pan and scrape all pan juices into the butter:

4 tbs butter

(3) Add, swirl around pan well to incorporate, pour over meat and serve immediately:

½ cup Marsala
salt and pepper to taste

VEAL CUTLETS IN CREAM

(1) Have pounded and cut into serving pieces:

1½ lbs veal cutlets

(2) Brown lightly in hot butter on both sides, remove from pan and keep warm:

3 tbs butter
the veal pieces

(3) Add to pan and reduce slightly:

½ cup sherry or Madeira

(4) Add, return meat to sauce, heat to just boiling and boil 1 minute:

½ cup heavy cream
6 fresh tarragon leaves or ½ tsp dried tarragon, soaked in the wine

(5) Serve with new potatoes and tiny green peas.

VEAL SCALLOPINI WITH PARMESAN CHEESE

(1) Have ready a wooden board, wooden mallet and:

> 2 lbs veal cutlets, cut 1 inch thick
> 1 cup grated Parmesan cheese
> salt and pepper to taste

(2) Spread a piece of waxed paper or butcher's paper on the board, put a piece of veal on the paper, sprinkle veal with cheese, salt and pepper and cover with a second piece of paper. Pound with the mallet until the meat is ½ inch thick and spread out. Turn meat, sprinkle second side with cheese, salt and pepper and pound until meat is ¼ inch thick or even slightly less. Cut meat into portions about as large as the palm of your hand. Repeat until all veal is pounded and cut.

(3) Brown scallopini on both sides in a wide heavy pan in:

> 2 tbs butter
> 2 tbs oil

(4) Add to pan, cover and simmer until tender, about 15 minutes:

> 1 cup dry white wine
> 1 cup beef or veal broth

(5) Sprinkle over scallopini and serve at once with sauce poured over:

> (3 tbs minced ham)
> 1 tbs lemon juice
> ¼ tsp each minced or dried oregano,
> thyme and marjoram
> 2 tbs chopped parsley
> 2 tbs grated Parmesan cheese

VEAL SCALLOPINI WITH MUSHROOMS

(1) Heat in a wide heavy pan until bubbling:

> 2 tbs butter
> 2 tbs olive oil

(2) Add and cook, stirring, for 3 minutes:

> 3 shallots, minced

(3) Add and brown quickly on both sides; if necessary, do in two batches and keep the cooked veal warm in a low oven:

> 1½ lbs veal, pounded and
> cut into serving pieces

(4) While the veal is cooking, sauté mushrooms gently in the oil and butter until just tender, about 6 minutes:

> 2 tbs oil
> 2 tbs butter
> ½ lb mushrooms, sliced thin

(5) When all the veal is cooked, and being kept warm in the oven, add to the pan in which the veal cooked:

> the sautéed mushrooms and cooking butter
> 1 cup heavy cream
> juice of ½ lemon
> salt and pepper to taste

(6) Let sauce boil for 1 minute, return veal to sauce and serve as soon as veal is again heated through and covered with the sauce. Serve with rice or noodles.

VEAL SCALLOPINI WITH LEMON

(1) Heat in a heavy pan until bubbling:
> 2 tbs butter
> 2 tbs olive oil

(2) Add and cook quickly until browned on both sides; cook in two batches if necessary, or cook in two heavy pans:
> 1½ lbs veal, pounded and
>   cut into serving pieces

(3) Remove veal and keep warm in a low oven. Add to butter remaining in pan and stir until smooth and browned:
> 2 tbs butter
> 2 tbs flour

(4) Add and stir until thickened:
> juice and grated rind of 1 lemon
> 1 lemon, sliced paper-thin
> ½ cup white wine

(5) Return veal to sauce, cook only until veal is coated with sauce and heated and serve immediately.

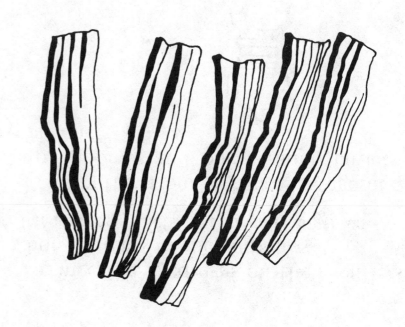

VEAL CUTLETS HOLSTEIN

(1) Divide into 6 pieces and season well:
1½–2 lbs veal cutlets, cut ½ inch thick

(2) Place veal cutlets between 2 sheets of butcher's or waxed paper and pound them to ¼-inch thickness with a wooden mallet, or have butcher pound them.

(3) In a heavy pan, fry cutlets until golden, about 10 minutes, turning once, in:
3 tbs butter
3 tbs lard

(4) Add, cover and simmer until tender, about 10 minutes:
½ cup beef broth

(5) In the meantime, fry in a second pan until done, season and trim:
2 tbs butter
6 eggs

(6) Arrange the fried eggs on the 6 cutlets on a hot platter. On the eggs cross:
6 flat anchovy fillets, cut in half lengthwise

(7) Pour butter from both pans together, heat to bubbling and pour around cutlets. Serve at once.

WIENER SCHNITZEL

(1) Divide into pieces and pound to ¼-inch thickness:

> 1½ lbs veal cutlet, cut ½ inch thick

(2) Dredge veal in a mixture of:

> ¼ cup flour
> ¼ tsp salt
> ⅛ tsp pepper

(3) Dip dredged schnitzel into:

> 2 beaten eggs

(4) Roll schnitzel in:

> 1½ cups bread crumbs

(5) Fry breaded schnitzel in butter in one or two pans. Butter in the pans should be deep enough to fry one side of meat at a time, about ⅛ inch deep:

> ½ cup butter, approximately

(6) Fry in the hot butter until golden, turning once. Serve on hot plates with lemon wedges.

LIVER WITH PEPPERS

(1) Dip in oil and broil for 2½–3 minutes on each side under high heat on an oiled rack:

    6 *½-inch-thick slices calves liver*

(2) On each liver slice place:

    ½-inch-thick red or green pepper rings

(3) Fill rings with:

    grated sharp cheese, approximately
    ½ cup in all

(4) Sprinkle over cheese and push under broiler until cheese melts:

    2 tsp paprika

(5) Serve at once with:

    1 jar heated spaghetti or tomato sauce

LIVER ON APPLE SLICES

(1) Dip in oil and broil quickly under high heat, then keep warm on a hot platter in a warm oven:

    6 thick onion slices, seasoned with
    salt and pepper
    6 thick slices peeled and cored apples, sugared

(2) Dip in oil and broil on an oiled rack under high heat for 2½–3 minutes on each side:

    6 slices calves liver, at least ½ inch thick

(3) At the same time, broil and drain:

    12 slices bacon

(4) Serve liver at once on apple slices, covered with onion slices and bacon.

Bacon may be broiled or fried ahead of time and laid on the liver for the last 2 minutes of broiling.

BROILED LIVER WITH ROSEMARY

(1) Dip in boiling water for a few seconds and draw off skins of:

> 6 very small tomatoes

(2) Cut lid off top of tomatoes and scoop out a little of the pulp. Fill tomatoes with a mixture of:

> ½ cup heavy cream, whipped
> ¼ cup well-drained or freshly ground horseradish
> ¼ cup freshly grated raw apple
> salt and pepper to taste

(3) Dip in oil and broil under high heat for 2½–3 minutes on each side on an oiled rack:

> 6 ½-inch-thick slices calves liver

(4) Season with:

> salt and pepper to taste
> 1 tsp crushed dried rosemary

(5) Serve at once on a hot platter with the filled tomatoes and mashed potatoes mixed with a little tomato juice.

HUNGARIAN PAPRIKA VEAL BALLS

(1) Mix and shape into 12 balls:
1½ lbs ground veal
1 medium onion, minced
1 egg beaten
1 can small white potatoes,
drained and diced, or
1½ cups diced cooked potatoes
2 tsp minced parsley
¼ tsp paprika
salt and pepper to taste

(2) In a wide pan, brown veal balls, shaking pan to brown evenly on all sides, in:
4 tbs butter

(3) Push meat balls to one side of the pan and stir into remaining butter until brown:
1–2 tsp paprika, or to taste

(4) Add, stir well and simmer, covered, for 12–15 minutes:
1 cup sour cream

(5) While the veal balls are cooking, prepare according to package directions and drain well:
½ lb medium noodles

(6) Take veal pan from heat, stir in and pour into center of noodles, arranged in a ring on a warmed platter:
½ cup sour cream

(7) Brown together quickly and pour over noodles and veal:
6 tbs butter
4 tbs bread crumbs

(8) Serve immediately, sprinkled with:
paprika to taste

VEAL KIDNEYS IN MUSTARD SAUCE

(1) Heat to bubbling in a heavy pan:
   4 tbs butter

(2) Add and turn gently in the butter for 10 minutes:
   4 veal kidneys, all fat and filaments removed

(3) Take out kidneys and keep them warm. To butter remaining in pan, add in order listed, cooking a moment between each addition:
   2 small shallots, minced
   6 tbs dry vermouth
   1 tbs lemon juice
   ½ tsp grated lemon rind

(4) Continue to cook until sauce is reduced to half, take from heat and stir in:
   2 tbs Dusseldorf or Dijon or
   any mild brown mustard

   2 tbs soft butter
   2 tbs minced parsley

(5) Slice kidneys paper-thin, return slices to sauce and set over low heat to warm kidneys. Do not boil.

(6) Serve at once over rice or with fingers of buttered toast.

SKEWERED LAMB

SHISH KABOBS IN THE KITCHEN OVEN

String fresh or marinated lamb and other ingredients on skewers and place skewers on broiler rack about 3 inches from the heat unit. Broil, basting and turning frequently, until browned. Allow about 18–20 minutes in all, depending on size of lamb chunks.

SHISH KABOBS ON OPEN COALS OR BARBECUE

Marinate in refrigerator, string on skewers and broil over coals, turning and basting frequently until browned and done. This method should take less time than oven broiling, but exact time depends on distance from coals. Test a piece of lamb after 15 minutes. The meat should be pink inside.

BASIC LAMB SHISH KABOB

(1) Have ready:
2 lbs lamb, cubed (and marinated)
1 green pepper, seeded and
cut into 1¼-inch squares
1 jar white onions
12 mushroom caps
small eggplant, peeled and cubed

(2) String on 6 skewers in this order: lamb cube, eggplant cube, green pepper square, lamb cube, mushroom cap, onion, lamb cube, eggplant cube, mushroom cap.

(3) Brush with melted butter and sprinkle with fresh or dried oregano and season to taste. Cook as described above.

MARINADE FOR KABOBS, OPTIONAL

Combine and use as a marinade:
½ cup dry sherry
½ cup apricot or pineapple juice
½ cup soy sauce
½ cup honey
½ tsp each ground cloves,
cinnamon and ginger
1 lemon, sliced paper-thin

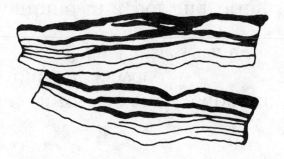

79

(1) Cook in a wide pan for 5 minutes, over medium heat, stirring constantly:
3 cups minced raw veal
½ cup butter

(2) Add, increase heat and cook 5 minutes longer:

¼ cup sherry

(3) Add, reduce heat and simmer 5 minutes longer:
2 8-ounce cans sliced mushrooms

(4) Add and cook until very hot and serve at once on hot toast or hot biscuits:
1 cup heavy cream
salt and pepper to taste

SKEWERED LAMB

(1) Cut into 1½-inch cubes and divide equally onto 6 skewers:

    2 lbs boneless lamb

(2) Combine in a pot and bring to a boil:

    9 tbs prune juice
    1½ tbs Worcestershire sauce
    ¼ cup brown sugar
    ¼ cup vinegar
    2 tsp salt
    pepper to taste
    3 tbs barbecue sauce

(3) Dip lamb in sauce and broil 3 inches from heat, turning every 4 minutes and basting each time with the sauce, for a total cooking time of 20 minutes.

(4) Serve immediately and pass remaining sauce separately.

HERBED LAMB CHOPS

(1) Place on broiler rack 3–4 inches from heat unit and broil 5 minutes:

    6 1-inch-thick loin lamb chops

(2) Turn with tongs and sprinkle with a mixture of the following:

    1 tsp dried rosemary, crushed
    1 tsp dried oregano, crushed
    1 tsp cut chives
    ¼ tsp garlic salt
    3 tsp lemon juice
    pepper and salt to taste

(3) Broil 5 minutes longer, or to desired doneness. Total broiling time should be no more than 10–12 minutes, and lamb should be brown on the outside and pink—not gray—on the inside.

HAWAIIAN LAMB BALLS

Preheat oven to 200°F.

(1) Combine, mix well and shape into small balls, about 1½ inches in diameter:

2 lbs ground lamb
2 egg yolks
1 medium onion, chopped fine
1 cup bread crumbs
1 tbs parsley
salt and pepper to taste

(2) Brown lamb balls in a wide heavy pan, shaking to brown evenly on all sides in butter, remove to warmed platter and keep hot in the oven:

3 tbs butter

(3) To butter remaining in pan, add and stir until jelly is melted:

1 tbs mint jelly
½ jar red currant jelly
1 small can pineapple chunks, drained
1 pinch ground cinnamon
1 pinch ground cloves

(4) Return lamb balls to sauce and swirl until well coated. Serve with rice or with picks as a cocktail appetizer.

MIXED GRILL WITH LAMB

(1) Broil on oiled rack 3–4 inches from heat unit for 8–10 minutes:

> 6 *1-inch thick rib lamb chops*

(2) Turn chops with tongs and add to rack:

> *3 tomatoes, halved, cut side up*
> *6 slices thick bacon*
> *6 ¼-inch-thick onion slices*
> *6 pork sausages*
> *6 slices canned yams*

(3) Brush chops and accompaniments, except bacon, with a mixture of:

> *4 tbs butter, melted*
> *½ clove garlic, crushed*
> *1 tbs minced parsley*
> *½ tsp rosemary or oregano*
> *salt and pepper to taste*

(4) Broil 5–6 minutes longer, brushing once more with above mixture and turning bacon and sausage and yams to brown both sides.

(5) Serve on very hot plates, dividing all things equally.

INDIAN CURRY LAMB BALLS

Preheat oven to 200°F.

(1) Combine, mix well and shape into small balls, about 1½ inches in diameter:

> 2 lbs ground lamb
> 2 egg yolks
> 1 medium onion, chopped fine
> 1 cup bread crumbs
> 1 tbs minced fresh mint or parsley or
> ½ tsp dried mint
> and 1 tbs parsley
> salt and pepper to taste

(2) Brown lamb balls in a wide heavy pan, shaking to brown evenly on all sides, in:

> 3 tbs butter

(3) Remove browned lamb balls and keep hot in the oven. To butter remaining in pan, add and stir until brown, then add cream and boil 1 minute:

> 1–2 tsp curry powder
> 1 cup heavy cream

(4) Return lamb balls to sauce, swirl until well coated and hot and serve immediately with rice or with picks as a cocktail appetizer. If lamb balls are to be used as an appetizer, make them smaller and make the sauce hotter by adding more curry powder.

MINTED LAMB CHOPS

(1) Melt over hot water in a double boiler:
> ½ jar mint jelly

(2) Arrange on an oiled broiler rack and brush with melted mint jelly:
> 6 1-inch-thick loin lamb chops

(3) Season with salt and pepper and broil 3–4 inches from heat unit for 5 minutes. Turn, brush with jelly, season and broil 5–6 minutes longer.

(4) Arrange chops on heated serving platter and keep warm in oven.

(5) To juices left in broiler pan add:
> remaining melted mint jelly
> ¼ cup water or bouillon
> 3 tbs minced mint leaves
> salt and pepper to taste

(6) Boil, stirring, for 1 minute, pour over chops and serve.

ITALIAN BROILED LAMB CHOPS

(1) Broil on oiled rack 3–4 inches from heat unit for 10 minutes:
> 6 1-inch-thick rib lamb chops

(2) Turn with tongs, brush with butter and broil 5 minutes longer:
> 3 tbs melted butter

(3) Brush again with remaining butter and sprinkle with:
> 6 tbs grated Parmesan cheese
> 1 pinch dried or fresh minced basil
> salt and freshly ground black pepper to taste

(4) Broil until cheese is browned, about 3 minutes, and serve hot with:
> 1 small can Italian tomato sauce, heated

CHICKEN

FRIED CHICKEN WINGS FOR A COCKTAIL PARTY APPETIZER

(1) Cut off wing tips and use to make broth. Cut through the second joint to separate each chicken wing into 2 parts. Arrange the thin first joints and the thick second joints in separate batches, as second joints require more frying time. Use in all:

2 lbs chicken wings, approx. 14 whole wings

(2) Prepare in a brown paper bag:

½ cup flour
1 tsp salt
¼ tsp pepper
(1 dash Dash)

(3) Add the chicken wings, in separate batches, and shake until well dredged.

(4) Dip dredged wings into:
2 eggs, beaten with 2 tbs water

(5) Roll wings in:

1½ cups dry bread crumbs

(6) Fry in deep fat, heated to 365°F until richly browned, about 7 minutes for the thin first joints and 9–10 minutes for the thicker second joints.

CHICKEN KIEV

(1) At least 3 hours before dinner, combine on waxed paper and shape into a long, thin roll and place in freezer:

8 tbs soft butter
4 shallots, minced or 4 tbs minced onion
2 tbs minced parsley
1 tbs minced chives
1 large clove garlic, crushed
salt to taste

(2) Pound thin with a mallet, between 2 pieces of waxed paper, without breaking:

12 half chicken breasts,
weighing about 8 ounces each

(3) Cut chilled butter into 12 sections and roll one into each half chicken breast. Turn in sides before rolling to completely envelop butter. Secure with wooden picks or kitchen string.

(4) Prepare in 3 separate bowls:

1 cup flour, sifted with 1 tsp salt
2 eggs, beaten with 2 tbs water
1 cup bread crumbs

(5) Dredge rolled chicken pieces with flour, dip in egg and roll in bread crumbs. Refrigerate them until 15 minutes before they are to be cooked.

(6) Brown breaded chicken rolls evenly in pan, about 15 minutes, in hot:

*½ cup **butter***
¼ cup lard or shortening

Remove picks or string and serve with vegetables and potatoes. The melted butter acts as a sauce; it runs out when the chicken is cut.

CHICKEN WITH ALMONDS

(1) Heat in a heavy pan over high heat:

4 tbs oil

1 tsp salt

(2) Add and cook 3 minutes:

3 cups raw diced chicken meat

(3) Stir in, in order listed, then simmer 4 minutes:

3 tbs soy sauce

1½ cups smallest green peas

1¼ cups diced celery

1 small can sliced mushrooms

1 cup boiling water

(4) Cover and cook 4 minutes longer.

(5) Combine, add to chicken and reduce heat:

*2 tbs cornstarch, **mixed with:***

½ cup cold water

(6) Allow to cook, without boiling, until thickened, then take from heat.

(7) Place everything in a shallow serving dish and sprinkle with:

¾ cup toasted almonds

Serve with rice.

FOURTEEN-MINUTE CHICKEN

(1) Sauté, stirring constantly for 3 minutes:
2½ lbs raw chicken meat,
cut in medium dice
4 tbs butter

(2) Add, cover and simmer 5 minutes longer:
2 medium onions, chopped
1 4-ounce can sliced mushrooms
1 package frozen tiny peas, thawed
and drained

(3) Add, increase heat, cover and cook 6 minutes longer:
1 10-ounce can condensed cream of
mushroom soup
1 10-ounce can tomatoes
2 chicken bouillon cubes
salt, if needed, after cubes have dissolved
water, if a more liquid sauce is preferred

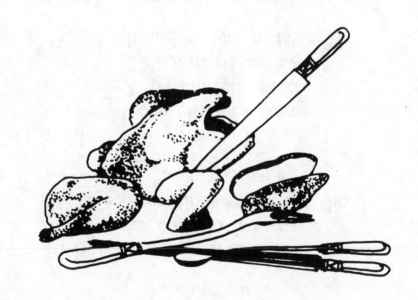

Serve with pre-cooked rice, white wine, warmed rolls and a soufflé for dessert.

CHICKEN WITH CUCUMBERS

(1) Sauté in very hot oil:
   2 cloves garlic, crushed
   ¼ cup oil

(2) Add and sauté 4 minutes:
   3 chicken breasts, boned and
   cut into small cubes

(3) Add, cover and cook 4 minutes longer:
   2 tbs soy sauce
   ½ tsp MSG
   2½ cups peeled and diced cucumber

(4) Stir in and cook until thickened, about 1 minute:
   1½ tbs cornstarch, dissolved in:
   6 tbs water

(5) Stir well and serve at once, sprinkled with:
   2 tbs freshly minced parsley

QUICK LIVER PATÉ

(1) Rub mixing bowl with cut side of:
   ½ clove garlic

(2) In bowl, mix until smooth:
   1 can chicken liver paste
   1 2-inch length liver sausage, diced
   1 tbs mayonnaise

(3) Add:
   ¼ cup chopped pecans
   2 tbs minced onion
   2 tbs minced parsley
   salt and pepper to taste

(4) Combine ingredients well and add:
   enough mayonnaise to make
   a spreadable pâté

If this is to be used as a "dip" instead of a spread, beat in more mayonnaise.

CHICKEN LIVER PATÉ

(1) Sauté until golden, over medium heat, about 5 minutes:

    2 tbs chopped onion
    ½ clove garlic, crushed
    4 tbs chicken fat or butter

(2) Add and sauté until lightly browned and still pink inside, about 3 minutes:

    1 lb chicken livers

(3) Add and press through sieve or blend until smooth:

    1 tsp salt
    ¼ tsp pepper

(4) Set pan in which livers cooked over medium heat and deglaze with:

    2 tbs brandy
    2 tbs sherry

(5) Stir contents of pan into livers, correct seasoning, fill into an earthenware crock and chill.

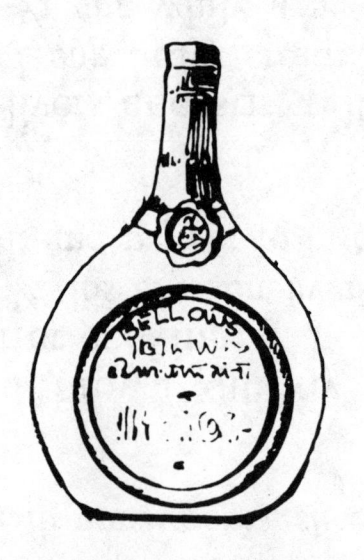

Serve with toasted or oven-dried bread rounds and cold seedless grapes.

FRENCH CHICKEN LIVERS

Preheat oven to 200°F.

(1) Sauté in a large heavy pan, over medium heat, for 4 minutes:

> 1 large onion, sliced
> 3 tbs butter

(2) Push onions aside and lightly brown on both sides:

> 2 large apples, peeled, cored and
> cut into large slices

(3) Mound onions on apple slices and set on a hot platter into oven to keep warm.

(4) Add butter to pan if necessary, and cook mushrooms until limp. Remove to platter in oven:

> (2 tbs butter)
> ½ lb mushrooms, sliced

(5) Add and brown quickly on all sides and season after cooking:

> 1½ lbs chicken livers
> salt and pepper to taste

(6) Add to livers and stir well:

> 1 cup heavy cream
> ½ cup white wine
> 1 pinch curry powder
> 1 pinch sugar
> 2 tbs chopped parsley

(7) Serve livers with the apple-onion slices as a garnish.

CHICKEN LIVERS MARGO

(1) Sauté over medium heat for 7 minutes:
    4 slices bacon, diced
    ½ cup chopped onions
    ¼ cup minced green peppers

(2) Add and brown on all sides for 5 minutes:
    1½ lbs chicken livers, dredged in flour
    ½ tsp dried thyme

(3) Add and cook 6 minutes longer:
    ¾ cup red wine
    ¾ cup pitted ripe olives
    ¼ cup chopped parsley
    salt and pepper to taste

Serve over buttered toast, rice or scrambled eggs.

CHICKEN LIVERS IN SOUR CREAM

(1) In a skillet, over medium heat, sauté for 3 minutes, turning with a wooden spoon:
>1½ lbs chicken livers
>4 tbs butter

(2) Add and cook 4 minutes longer:
>½ lb mushrooms, sliced or buttons

(3) Add and flame immediately:
>⅓ cup brandy, warmed

(4) When flame dies down, reduce heat under pan to very low. Beat together and stir into livers in pan, making sure not to boil:
>1 cup sour cream
>2 egg yolks
>½ tsp salt, or to taste
>¼ tsp pepper, or to taste

(5) Sprinkle with:
>2 tbs chopped chives or parsley

Serve over hot buttered toast or rice.

INDEX